LOST BENEATH THE ICE

Dated October 8, 1850, this dramatic painting by
Lieutenant Gurney Cresswell shows *Investigator*
trapped in ice and dwarfed by massive floes.

LOST
BENEATH
THE ICE

THE STORY OF HMS *INVESTIGATOR*

Text by Andrew Cohen
Images Selected by Parks Canada

DUNDURN
TORONTO

Project Editor: Diane Young
Editors: Bob Chodos, Ginny Freeman MacOwan, Susan Joanis
Design: Courtney Horner
Printer: Friesens

Library and Archives Canada Cataloguing in Publication

Cohen, Andrew, 1955-, author
    Lost beneath the ice : the story of HMS Investigator
/ by Andrew Cohen.

Issued in print and electronic formats.
ISBN 978-1-4597-1949-1

    1. Arctic regions--Discovery and exploration. 2. Northwest
Passage--Discovery and exploration. 3. Search and rescue operations--
Arctic regions. 4. Investigator (Ship). 5. Franklin, John, 1786-1847--
Travel--Arctic regions. I. Title.

G660.C64 2013   919.804   C2013-902966-4
                                              C2013-902967-2

1   2   3   4   5   17   16   15   14   13

We acknowledge the support of the **Canada Council for the Arts** and the **Ontario Arts Council** for our publishing program. We also acknowledge the financial support of the **Government of Canada** through the **Canada Book Fund** and **Livres Canada Books**, and the **Government of Ontario** through the **Ontario Book Publishing Tax Credit** and the **Ontario Media Development Corporation**.

Care has been taken to trace the ownership of copyright material used in this book. The author and the publisher welcome any information enabling them to rectify any references or credits in subsequent editions.

J. Kirk Howard, President

The publisher is not responsible for websites or their content unless they are owned by the publisher.

Printed and bound in Canada.

Visit us at
Dundurn.com | @dundurnpress
Facebook.com/dundurnpress | Pinterest.com/Dundurnpress

Dundurn	Gazelle Book Services Limited	Dundurn
3 Church Street, Suite 500	White Cross Mills	2250 Military Road
Toronto, Ontario, Canada	High Town, Lancaster, England	Tonawanda, NY
M5E 1M2	LA1 4XS	U.S.A. 14150

C O N T E N T S

PART ONE

INVESTIGATOR LOST

———————

TRAPPED IN ICE

September 9, 1852. WITH SUMMER NOT YET OVER and autumn not yet begun, the ice — that awful, damnable, imperishable ice — had still not relented, relaxed, or retreated. It had held HMS *Investigator* fast in its grip for a year. By all laws of decency, it should have released Her Majesty's Ship and its sixty-six embattled souls some time ago. Had nature been so inclined, they would have been on their way home by now to England, the impossibly green isle they had left so hopefully two years, eight months, and eleven days ago.

But here they remained, fixed in the ice, inert and useless, precisely where they had been since September 1851. For twelve hard months, they had been held captive on the shores of the Polar Sea: latitude 74 degrees north, longitude 117.54 degrees west. When they sailed into this sheltering cove, where Captain Robert McClure had decided to spend the winter — a decision questioned by officers then and historians

now — he named it Bay of God's Mercy, "in grateful acknowledgement of the Lord's wonderful help."

To be sure, Mercy Bay, as it became known, had delivered them from the dangers of the murderous ice pack in the open sea. But a year later few saw this bleak, grey footprint of frozen water, with its long sandbar, as merciful. In fact, it represented instead a cruel irony. Alexander Armstrong, the ship's surgeon, bitterly recalled: "It would have been *a mercy had we never entered it.*" By September 1852, *Investigator* had not only been paralyzed for a whole year, but it was becoming clear — given the advancing calendar, the gathering cold, and the swelling ice — that it would be here for *another* winter. Mercy Bay? For this misbegotten ship, bad enough that a refuge had become a prison. Now, in the jaws of another deep freeze, it threatened to become its grave.

For Captain McClure and his crew, this was the critical moment in their long, unprecedented voyage through the Arctic Ocean. Having wintered here successfully, surviving the long, dark, cold days in relatively good cheer, they had expected that the ice would break up, the sea would open, and they would sail east. This was a reasonable expectation, even in the Arctic. Even here, spring *does* follow winter, albeit grudgingly, and summer *does* follow spring, usually.

But by the end of June 1852, as the temperature reached a balmy 35 degrees Fahrenheit (2°C), things were not happening as they should. The ice was seven feet, two inches (2.15 m) thick, which was three inches (8 cm) *more* than the previous month. A year earlier, the ice depth had been two feet (60 cm) less. By July, the temperature had finally reached 4 degrees (2°C) above freezing, and the falling snow was melting. The land was soaked, a canvas of waterfalls, pools, and rivulets. On July 31, Johann Miertsching, a missionary, noted in his journal that "the weather is consistently bad and very foggy; in the cold, dark winter months we had a cloudless sky all the time; now in the summer we have for the most part impenetrable clouds over us instead of sun; also by day a thick mist rises from the land."

This meant that by late summer there was no real thaw, leaving the sailors waiting forlornly for their release. It wasn't coming. Every day a seaman climbed the 800-foot (250-m) bluff nearby to gaze at Viscount Melville Sound and surveyed the sea, looking for open water. Every day, he returned with the same grim report: "No break-up. No movement in the ice."

On board *Investigator*, conditions were deteriorating. With nothing much to do, the men were bored to distraction. There was little wildlife to hunt anymore; all but the birds had departed. The men were too weak from malnutrition for athletics; Miertsching noted that hunger takes "all the joy out of men, even the desire to live." On August 2, he said the fog had produced "a sorrowful and gloomy frame of mind."

On August 10, a seaman was caught stealing bread; as punishment he received three dozen lashes from the cat o' nine tails. This was how the captain maintained discipline among the unruly seamen, an approach that some have noted was harsher than that of most of his counterparts. Unsurprisingly, it did not endear him to his men.

By August 21, there was still no discernible change in the ice. However, in preparation for their day of deliverance, the ice around the ship had been blasted away with an ample supply of gunpowder brought along for this purpose. The crew anticipated that any day the ship would be carried out with the tide, when the ice broke up. Hopes rose when a strip of water 50 feet (15 m) across appeared along the beach, necessitating a small boat to reach the land when coming from the ship. To keep them occupied, the men were told to fish, which they did, catching 173 little fish of unknown species. Then, cruelly and quickly, the opening in the ice closed up again.

On August 29, the maximum temperature was 32 degrees Fahrenheit (0°C), the minimum just 21 degrees (-6°C). Miertsching said there was still a hope — "unhappily, a feeble one" — that they would reach England that year. The reality was that there was new ice along the beach three inches (8 cm) deep, so thick that some of the crew had been skating on it for two days. New snow had fallen. The men were becoming more dispirited; they walked about with "drooping heads and empty stomachs." The missionary reported that a young sailor named Mark Bradbury had been put under watch for the previous three days; he was "distracted" and made "a terrible noise at night," wrote Miertsching. Translation: He's going mad.

No wonder the captain, heavy with anxiety, was taking long, solitary walks along the bluffs. While he tried to be optimistic around the men, he was deeply worried. Miertsching observed that sighs and prayers would come from his cabin, expressions of consuming anxiety and inner turmoil. He noted that the telltale sounds said "much more than he reveals in words." On September 3, the little water they had seen the previous month was frozen again. Hour by hour, they watched and waited, praying in vain for a break in the ice. "Everyone has despaired of reaching England this year," he wrote.

Now it was the morning of September 9. On his last walk, the captain had considered the situation carefully. He had made some critical decisions, as a captain must. It was clear to him that the ice was not melting. It was equally clear that the situation was dire. The men, having subsisted on two-thirds rations for a year, were weak. Without fruit and vegetables, scurvy was setting in, bringing its own order of anguish. There had been some progress warding it off by eating sorrel pulled from the barren tundra. The crew was also containing its hunger with meat from game killed on the land. But both sources of nourishment were running out. The surgeon had warned the captain that he could not expect the men to last another year. Those who didn't die would go crazy. Isolated, cold, hungry, and depressed, *Investigator*'s seamen were without comfort, hope, or purpose.

McClure gathered the crew on the upper deck and delivered what Miertsching called "a solemn and impressive speech." It was part sermon and part pep-talk:

He declared frankly that the ice would not break up this summer, and therefore they would be compelled to pass a second winter in the same place; he will do everything in his power to make their lives throughout the long winter as pleasant and comfortable as possible, and he urged them not to lose heart, but with firm faith to trust in God, under Whose protection they were, to discipline ourselves and behave like British seamen, whose steadfast courage had never failed; for himself, he had a firm conviction that not one of us would be left behind, but they would safely reach their fatherland.

Then, from McClure, more heavy tidings: the daily food ration was to be reduced again, though the captain would share his personal store of food (officers had their own provisions) with the crew. This would allow them to remain in "good health," he said. According to the plan, the following spring he would order forty men to leave the ship. Eight would go to the Mackenzie River, seeking relief from a Hudson's Bay trading post in the region. Others would go to Port Leopold at Prince Regent's Inlet, where food and supplies had been stored by a ship on another mission. The rest of the crew would stay with the ship and sail it home when conditions permitted.

The captain was making an agonizing decision. What he had really decided, though he didn't spell it out, was to divide the crew, instituting a kind of triage. The weakest would go on a dangerous voyage over some 600 miles (1,000 km) to Cape Spencer, through Baffin Bay to Greenland in a small boat. It was an implausible journey. So was the prospect of those men finding their way home to England through the wilds of North America. Both would be hard enough in the best of times, but as the surgeon noted, in eight months' time, weakened by another winter spent on the ice, the men would be even more depleted. Was the captain serious about this?

There was a chance that the men would be rescued the next spring, as they hoped, when the Admiralty in London would surely dispatch a rescue expedition. More likely, they would continue to struggle. There would not be provisions enough to sustain all sixty-six of them.

Of course, the game might return, and the temperature might rise. In his account of the voyage published in 1856, based on his journal and logbooks, Captain McClure wrote that his plan

> was cheerfully received by this excellent body of men; and those who thought they would be the first to go home, were soon speculating, with praiseworthy generosity, upon immediately volunteering to come out again in the first ship to the rescue of their messmates, and with light-hearted jocularity promising to bring them out a good stock of tobacco pipes .... With such men, and such spirit, all the difficulties and hardships before them vanished, and none repined at what Providence had sent them.

That was McClure's cheerful reading of the mood years later, which was as unpersuasive as the rest of his self-serving account. Miertsching, for his part, offered a more sober view: "One could observe many gloomy and anxious faces, but in this situation there was nothing to do but submit."

This then, was the fate of *Investigator* on September 9, 1852, a moment of existential crisis. Despite the captain's brave front, he doubted that all his men would survive until the next spring. They would make all necessary preparations for a second winter aboard the frozen ship, such as insulating the ship with thick banks of snow and ice. But they would face less food, failing health, and unrelenting anxiety. In the meantime, they would plan their unlikely escape the following spring. Until then, there would be numbing cold, gnawing hunger, painful isolation, and unbroken darkness. If there was any mercy left in the blue ice of Mercy Bay, these embattled souls would need every ounce of it.

THE AGE OF
ARCTIC EXPLORATION

HOW HAD IT COME TO THIS? HOW DID *INVESTIGATOR* and its spirited crew find themselves frozen in the ice of the Arctic in the middle of the nineteenth century? What mix of ambition, daring, madness, and romance could draw this thrusting captain, his cynical surgeon, a goodhearted missionary, and a crew of roughhewn, roughhousing sailors to the most remote, bleak, harsh, and unknown place on earth in a wooden sailing ship? And more than a century and a half later, what would compel a raft of historians, archaeologists, and scientists — living in that Northland now called Canada — to chronicle the ship's journey, contemplate its motives, explore its mission, and most importantly, launch an expedition to find its physical remains in the depths of the Arctic Sea? The fundamental reason — at least in regard to the recent expedition — is that the captain and crew of *Investigator* were the first to be recognized for discovering a northwest passage, the fabled route from Europe to Asia through the northern waters of North America.

What motivated them to try? Finding the much-heralded passage would mean avoiding the long voyage around South America — or so it was hoped. Explorers had sought the route for centuries, but none with the determination of the British in the nineteenth century. For geographers, the Northwest Passage was the greatest mystery of its day. For seafarers, it was the greatest prize. Both knew that it promised celebrity and money: a prize of £10,000 had been offered by the British Parliament, about $1 million in today's value.

An incentive for the modern crew was the historic contact the original crew had — both directly and indirectly — with the Inuit peoples of the area. Prior to 1851, other explorers had come into contact with different groups of Copper Inuit located on the mainland, typically near the mouth of the Coppermine River. In May and June of 1851, McClure and the crew of *Investigator* encountered Inuit in the vicinity of Minto Inlet, representing the first European contact with the

Inuit of Victoria Island. These were likely Kangiryuarmiut (people of Prince Albert Sound, a group of the Copper Inuit). While this encounter was relatively brief, the material influence stemming from this group's subsequent access to the cache site left by the crew at Mercy Bay would be much longer lived. The Kangiryuarjatmiut (people of Minto Bay, another closely related group of the Copper Inuit) also made repeated forays from Victoria Island to Mercy Bay to quarry materials from the cache. These Inuit on Victoria Island, because of their "extreme isolation … were among the very last Canadian Inuit groups to be contacted by the outside world."

For all that though, and unique as it is, the story of *Investigator* resonates today because it is both historic and human. For Canadians, it is very much *our* story. It is a tale of ambition, deceit, daring, guile, fortune, endurance, success, and failure. It is sown with suffering and sadness. Even more, it is rich with irony. *Investigator* unlocked the mystery of the Northwest Passage only to find that it was impassable, with no practical or commercial value in the 1850s. Ultimately, the captain found fortune and fame. In winning the prize, though, he lost his ship, some of his crew, and much of his honour.

To understand *Investigator,* we must recall the age. With the end of the Napoleonic Wars at the Battle of Waterloo in 1815, a new chapter in polar exploration began. While Martin Frobisher, Henry Hudson, and William Baffin had searched out the basins of Hudson Bay and Baffin Bay in the sixteenth and seventeenth centuries, they had concluded that neither would lead them to that much-coveted western channel to the East Indies.

As historian Leslie H. Neatby writes, for the next two centuries there were only fitful and ultimately unsuccessful efforts to challenge the theory. Well into the second decade of the nineteenth century, the northeastern and northern shores of North America, from Repulse Bay to the Bering Strait, were a mystery, except for the mouths of the Coppermine and Mackenzie rivers. "Of the vast and complex archipelago that lay beyond, nothing at all was known except for some sections of the east shore of Baffin Island," writes Neatby. It was *terra incognita* — as mysterious to mariners then as the heavens would be to astronauts a century later.

Of course, any vacuum — political or natural — cries to be filled. Enter Great Britain. Of all the world's powers, it was best positioned to explore the Arctic after 1815. "Britain had emerged from the Napoleonic Wars relatively unscathed," writes author Shelagh D. Grant, "creating a serious logistics problem for the Admiralty."

At the height of the wars, the British Navy had 773

ships, 4,000 officers, and 140,000 sailors. Peace brought not a dividend but a penalty; many of its sailors were let go, creating a pool of seasoned yet unemployed seafarers. Those who remained in the navy had little to do. To John Barrow, the influential Second Secretary of the Admiralty, the answer was scientific research and polar exploration. He dreamed of discovering the Northwest Passage and reaching the North Pole; actually, it became an *idée fixe* for him. That he imagined the pole as a rock surrounded by open water scarcely mattered; this proud, hawk-nosed patrician, who would make polar exploration his obsession for more than three decades, was determined to know what was there, and he committed the men and ships at his command to find out. Here was a fortuitous meeting of curiosity, opportunity, and vanity.

And so began what Neatby calls "the grand epic of British discovery in the North American Arctic." In this, the voyage of *Investigator* in the first half of the 1850s was the critical but penultimate chapter. It came thirty-two years after Barrow's first polar missions. In 1818, he had sent two expeditions to the Arctic. One, led by Captain John Buchanan and Lieutenant John Franklin, sought the North Pole. The other, led by Captain John Ross and Lieutenant William Parry, sought the Northwest Passage. Both failed. In 1819, Parry led another expedition in search of the passage. He went to Melville Island, named after the admiral, and wintered at the appropriately named Winter Harbour. All would become guideposts on this new frozen frontier.

Parry's observations would guide McClure and *Investigator* a generation later. Parry published his journal, and so did Ross; their passionate language describing the perils of the region stirred great public interest in the Arctic back at home. In the popular mind, the Arctic was coming in from the cold, and that encouraged other fortune-seekers, of a sort, to head north. Shelagh Grant writes:

> The Admiralty expeditions launched the era of the venerated polar explorer, the epitome of manliness and virtue, usually victorious in overcoming seemingly insurmountable challenges, and bestowing honour and prestige on his country.

Increasingly, the motivation of polar exploration was less science than egotism. It was competition; it was to be first. It was about planting the flag in the ice and snow, staking a claim for Great Britain, however empty this wasteland. It was about King (later Queen) and Country. This is what drove these expeditions over the next three decades. Parry went out yet again in 1821 to look for the passage. Barrow sent out four more expeditions in the 1820s, which helped chart its contours. Exploration slowed in the 1830s (though there was a mission in 1836) and into the 1840s. By then Barrow was eighty years old.

Still determined to find the passage, he successfully petitioned the prime minister for money. Another expedition was established to sail into Lancaster Sound and head southwest, searching for the passage. Two ships, HMS *Terror* and HMS *Erebus*, under sail and steam, were provisioned with supplies for three years. Manned by 128 sailors, they attracted much attention when they set sail in 1845. Arctic fever was raging in England. The ships were under the command of Sir John Franklin, one of the most celebrated explorers of his day.

Franklin, knighted for his earlier Arctic exploits, was fifty-nine years old. While experienced, he was also fat and ungainly; some thought him unfit for sea. His ultimate appointment as leader of the expedition was due, in part, to his fiercely ambitious wife, Lady Jane Franklin, who was herself an adventurer and traveller. She was her husband's greatest advocate.

But when nothing was heard of Franklin by late 1847, the Admiralty worried. As historian Martin W. Sandler notes, captains always came back from the Arctic (even if they did not always return with their ships.) Now there were no captain and no ships, and it was a calamity at home. Tens of thousands of worshippers filled churches across England, and the effort to find Franklin became a *cause célèbre*. A massive international effort was launched, aided and financed by wealthy Americans as well as Britons. It "was the greatest activity the Arctic would ever witness," says Sandler. Over the next dozen years, some forty ships and 2,000 officers and men would join the search for Franklin, making this "the longest and most expensive search and rescue operation ever undertaken." Between 1848 and 1853, some twenty-eight expeditions on sea and land were sent to the Arctic. In 1850 alone, six expeditions were dispatched.

The first of these involved *Investigator* and HMS *Enterprise*. In another of the rich ironies of this saga, what began as a rescue mission for Captain McClure and his crew would ultimately end as one, though surely not as they had anticipated. Neither *Investigator* nor any other expedition would ever find Franklin, *Terror,* or *Erebus* (a challenge the government of Canada took up in 2008, when it launched a multiyear expedition to find the lost ships). Franklin had simply disappeared. Rather than McClure coming to the aid of Franklin, others would come to the aid of McClure. In this story, the rescuers became the rescued.

INVESTIGATOR'S JOURNEY

At 6:00 a.m. on January 20, 1850, *Investigator* set sail from Plymouth. She accompanied *Enterprise*. The two ships had returned the previous November from the Arctic, where they had spent eighteen months. They had tried to enter the Arctic from the east in 1848, but found the ice impenetrable. With no sign of Franklin, the ships were ordered to refit and restock back in England and chart a new course to the Polar Sea. This time the ships — the Admiralty generally sent ships in pairs, so that one could help if the other got into trouble — would approach from the west, through the Pacific Ocean.

This plan meant sailing south from England, navigating the treacherous waters of Cape Horn, sailing up the west coast of South America, and making for Honolulu Harbour in the Sandwich Islands (now Hawaii), a voyage of more than 10,000 miles (16,000 km). Then, after resupplying, *Investigator* would sail north around the Aleutian Islands, extending like a string of pebbles over a thousand miles (1,600 km), and into the Bering Strait. The mission, writes Neatby, was to search for Franklin "on the Alaska shore and the unknown seas of the western Arctic." As we know, *Investigator* never did find a trace of Franklin, his men, or his ships, but it did follow that shore and explore those waters, on land (dragging sledges) as well as on sea. In the end, that journey of discovery became its legacy.

The saga of *Investigator* is as much about its men as its mission. Its officers were perceptive, articulate, and opinionated. They recorded their thoughts and impressions in diaries and journals and published them afterward. To their detailed observations we owe what we know today of the expedition, both good and bad. None of them was a disinterested observer; indeed, some accounts are self-serving and uncritical. In one case, a diary was reconstructed after the fact, from other diaries.

The *dramatis personae* in this story begin with Robert John Le Mesurier McClure. He had sailed on that recent mission to the Arctic with Captain James Ross, as well as a disastrous earlier one in 1836. Now he would be captain of *Investigator* and second-in-command to Captain Richard Collinson of *Enterprise*, who was called dour and cautious. McClure, forty-two, was solitary, taciturn, and brooding. He was also sly, daring, self-assured, and competitive. "Although most Arctic explorers were ambitious," writes historian Pierre Berton, "McClure's ambitions were more naked and less admirable. There is little doubt that McClure was out for McClure first, and everybody else second." Beyond serving on the two polar missions, Neatby notes, McClure "was otherwise undistinguished." He had a protuberant nose, thick black hair, long sideburns, and a heavy beard characteristic of men of a certain station in Victorian England.

McClure was more than commander of *Investigator*; on his ship, far from home, he was master and emperor, the author of all fortune. On his judgment turned questions of life and death. To his crew, he was both benefactor and disciplinarian, who equally displayed acts of generosity and fits of anger. Berton calls him "unstable" and given to "spasms of uncontrollable fury." He made many decisions that led his critics to question his wisdom and, occasionally, his morality.

If McClure had a friend in this friendless precinct — perhaps a confidant or companion — it was Johann August Miertsching. A missionary of the Moravian Church, Miertsching was not a naval officer; he joined the expedition as an interpreter. In the 1840s, he had been a missionary on the coast of Labrador, where he preached Christianity and absorbed the language and customs of the Inuit. He eschewed wool uniforms (he wasn't a member of the navy anyway) for Inuit dress. In 1849, he was recruited to join McClure's expedition as interpreter to translate native tongues, though he spoke little English. Miertsching, thirty-two, was born in Saxony. He was kind, decent, sensitive, and well liked by everyone. The voyage, however, would test his tolerance and his faith.

The third of the prominent figures among the crew was the ship's surgeon, Alexander Armstrong. At thirty-one, he had achieved early distinction in the natural sciences. "He was shrewd, observant, much the best informed man on board, endowed with a gift for making those qualities unpalatable to his associates," writes Neatby. An unreconstructed skeptic, he was keenly aware, at all times, of the health of the crew. He knew more than anyone else what the men could endure, and on this voyage it was usually no more. His empathy brought him into conflict with McClure, whom Armstrong thought too ready to put his ambitions above his crew's welfare. Theirs was an uneasy relationship. Over the course of four years, Armstrong developed a deep distrust of McClure and his judgment, a smouldering resentment that Armstrong would take to his memoir, which portrays McClure caustically.

Beyond the captain, the surgeon, and the missionary, there were fifty-seven sailors and six officers on board *Investigator* when it entered the Arctic (it had left England with sixty-four men). The ship was neither old nor handsome, but it was strong. Built as a merchant vessel in 1848 at Greenock, Scotland, it was a barque with three masts rigged with square sails and a copper bottom, which had been added in 1849. It displaced 422 tons (430 tonnes) and measured 118 feet by 28 feet (36 m x 8.5 m). Purchased into the Royal Navy, it was immediately adapted for the Arctic in a shipyard near London. The hull planking was doubled with English oak, Canadian elm, and African teak. The bow and stern had been reinforced with timber and iron, the better to resist the teeth of the polar ice.

GETTING THERE

THINGS DIDN'T START WELL. EN ROUTE TO HAWAII, the crew was loud, disorderly, and often drunk, behaviour that shocked the pious Miertsching. Just four days after setting sail, on January 24, the ship was hit by a ferocious gale, which snapped its upper masts. Four men were swept overboard and then rescued. Rain and rough seas persisted for some time. A quarrel erupted between the captain and the officers.

Miertsching didn't understand much English — his diary was translated from German by Neatby in the 1960s — and the language barrier isolated him. Sea water filled his cabin, drenching his books and guitar. The dancing and noise made him feel so wretched (though not seasick) that he could scarcely control his feelings. *Investigator* had been at sea less than a month, and he already had misgivings. Miertsching knew this was not going to be an afternoon cruise on the Thames River, but he hadn't expected this level of rowdiness. As he left for the Arctic, he reflected on the dangers of the voyage. "Shall we see England or Europe again?" he asked. "When?" He mused about being away "perhaps for two years, perhaps for ever. The future is wrapped in obscurity." Later, as they made their way toward Hawaii, the question for him became which was more unbearable: the tropical heat or the oversexed crew, whom Miertsching called "these brazen sinners ... devils." There was an arrest every day, and someone was in confinement all the time. On April 6, Miertsching told of one of the crew receiving a punishment of four dozen lashes from the cat o' nine tails. Miertsching didn't object. (Neatby notes that liberal use of the lash was McClure's peculiar way; it was a far less common practice among captains on other polar expeditions.)

The ship made its way through the Strait of Magellan, rounded the Cape, and sailed up the west coast of South America, the Andes of Patagonia on its starboard side. The weather turned bad again, a third of the crew was sick, and life was miserable. On May 15, *Investigator* lost its top-masts in a squall, and the ship itself was nearly lost. The captain exploded at the first officer, Lieutenant William Haswell, who had left the deck. In a fury, McClure had him arrested, which he soon regretted, admitting later that he had not handled it "as a sincere Christian should have done."

On July 1, 1850, they reached Hawaii. *Investigator* had been at sea almost six months and had sailed 10,000 miles (16,000 km), already a spectacular voyage. They were supposed to stay a fortnight, restoring themselves and repairing the ship. But McClure soon learned that HMS *Enterprise* — its speedier counterpart, from which it had become separated — had waited just four days in Honolulu for *Investigator* and departed in frustration the day before. McClure also learned that if *Investigator* didn't catch up, *Enterprise* would commandeer HMS *Plover*, a supply ship anchored in the Bering Strait, to accompany it on its rescue mission into the Arctic. The message left by Captain Collinson for Captain McClure was clear: get to the Bering Strait (between Alaska and Siberia) posthaste, or risk being left behind. If he was not wanted on the voyage, McClure knew, his dreams of finding the Northwest Passage would evaporate like a soft summer mist. In a fury, McClure cut short his stay, forgave Haswell his mistakes, and put out to sea after four days.

To make up time, McClure took the first of several risks on this fateful voyage. Rather than sailing to the west, skirting around the reefs, the shallows, and the deep fog of the uncharted Aleutian Islands, he elected to cut right through them. As far as they knew, no European had done that. It worked. *Investigator* arrived in Kotzebue Sound on July 29 and found *Plover* but not *Enterprise*. Having taken the long way, *Enterprise* was now days behind *Investigator*.

McClure, the supreme opportunist, now saw his chance to get a jump on *Enterprise*. He told Captain Henry Kellet, his superior in command of HMS *Herald*, which was also in the area, that *Enterprise* was actually ahead of him, not behind, and he must therefore depart right away. Captain Kellet asked him to wait another day; McClure refused. "Cannot wait," he signalled. Although the ships were to travel in pairs when they could and although he knew that the sister ship had not come and gone, McClure sailed away. The other captain knew that McClure was lying but didn't stop him. This meant *Investigator* would go on to the Arctic on its own, without the benefit of a companion ship. In making this momentous decision, McClure was dishonest and reckless. He was consumed by ambition.

Alone, *Investigator* sailed through the Bering Strait, around Point Barrow in Alaska (then Russian territory) and along the coast. This was entirely new. "No ship had ever been where our ship now was," exclaimed Miertsching. Here they came into contact with Inuit, who were warm, affectionate, and bedazzled by the crew, having never seen Europeans before. Miertsching, proving his value as interpreter, spoke their language, which he had learned in Labrador. He offered them gifts and spoke to them of God.

The ship sailed through Cape Bathurst and Franklin Bay, framed by cliffs. They came to Banks Island, which McClure christened "Baring Land." He was naming it after Baring, the First Lord of the Admiralty, not realizing that it was the "Banks Land" first discovered by Parry. Snow, rain, and fog were common, as were monstrous pieces of ice, which often slowed the ship's progress. Sometimes the ice pack pushed the ship in the wrong direction, but *Investigator* was still moving.

Finally, on September 21, something happened. Although they were now frozen in the ice, *Investigator* was still being carried to the north. "If only it would keep going through Barrow Strait (Viscount Melville Sound) to Melville Island!" enthused Miertsching. If so, that would complete the Northwest Passage. McClure believed that the elusive ribbon of water flowing northeast was the missing link in the passage. He wondered, "Can it be that so humble a creature as I am will be permitted to perform what has baffled the talented and wise for hundreds of years?" Captain Parry had reached as far as Melville Island in 1819 and hibernated in Winter Harbour. Parry had approached that point from the Atlantic; here McClure was approaching it from the Pacific. Like Moses gazing upon the Promised Land from the heights but unable to enter it, McClure believed he was seeing the passage, even if he could not actually sail through it. Still, he knew in the marrow of his congealed, seafaring bones that beyond Barrow Strait was Melville Island.

From McClure, though, there was no sense of triumph that day. It was not for another month — after *Investigator* was battered, nearly broken, and locked in the polar ice for its first winter — that he would announce his discovery. It wasn't enough to see it, as they thought, from the top of the crow's nest on September 20, and again from the top of a mountain on October 10. He would have to stand on its shores. They were getting closer, though. The morning of

October 26, 1850, was "fine and cloudless." McClure, accompanied by a small party, had left the ship five days earlier to set out on the land, seeking the passage. Before sunrise they started up a hill, some 600 feet (180 m), which would, in the words of McClure, link "their discovery with those of Sir Edward Parry."

Imagine, if we can, the level of suspense and sheer anticipation for those stout Britons as they climbed that hill and awaited the light to expose the landscape, like a darkened photograph in a tray of developing fluid. As the sun rose, the panorama revealed itself, slowly and joyously. To the north, across the entrance of Prince of Wales Strait, were the frozen waters of Melville Strait. There it was. The land, the charts, the sense of things just told him that. "The Northwest Passage was discovered!" declared McClure in his memoir. "All doubt as to the water communication between the two great oceans was removed." All that was left, as McClure noted, was "to perfect the work by traversing the few thousand miles of known ground between them and their homes."

As McClure recalled, there was great happiness, but "no arrogant self-estimation formed part of the crowd of tumultuous feelings, which made their hearts beat so high, and never from the lips of man burst a more fervent *Thank God!*" At this point in his narrative McClure noted that, if Franklin and his crew should never be discovered, he (McClure) "nevertheless should not return to [his] country with empty hands."

GETTING STUCK

OVER THE NEXT FOUR YEARS, UNTIL MCCLURE and his crew finally returned to England on October 4, 1854, the question was not whether they would return with empty hands but whether they would return at all. As Wellington said of victory over Napoleon at the Battle of Waterloo, "it was a close-run thing." That they would not save John Franklin, who had no doubt perished long before they arrived, was clear early on; for the rest of their polar sojourn, they wondered whether they could save themselves. As much as the saga of *Investigator* from the autumn of 1850 revolves around McClure's dogged, dubious efforts to navigate the passage by sea (unsuccessful) and his expeditions to Melville Island by land (successful), it was something more. Fundamentally, it is the story of survival, which is as fascinating now as it was then.

By the time *Investigator* was imprisoned in the winter of 1850–51, with temperatures reaching -60 degrees Fahrenheit (-51°C), the crew had endured enough gales, squalls, storms, accidents, and missteps to understand perfectly the precariousness of their situation. The greatest danger, of course was the ice — ubiquitous, colossal, capricious, rapacious, unsentimental. Packs of ice floated about the Polar Sea like wolves in hot pursuit of prey, eager to crush *Investigator* to pieces. Floes and fragments were everywhere. There were bergs three times the size of the ship. While some historians say Miertsching exaggerated the travails of Arctic exploration, the terror of the ice is striking in paintings and chronicles of Victorian England. In the Arctic, a century and a half ago, there were multiple shades of white and even more shapes of ice. Ice was never friendly. Through nineteenth-century eyes, it was always sinister and terrifying, promising danger.

For crews unused to the North, in particular, it is hard to overstate the threat. On repeated occasions the men fully expected the ice to crush them; the ship groaned and whined as joints parted and oakum oozed from its seams. In the iron grip of the ice, it was not unusual for the men to transfer tons of provisions to the deck, or to wooden boats, and prepare to abandon ship, as happened on August 29, 1851. "This is the end," declared McClure, persuaded that it was. "The ship is breaking up." Miertsching called it "the most awful moment of our lives." Both assessments seemed to be true at the moment they were uttered. But then, like the captain's furies and the Arctic's wind, the crisis passed.

By the fall of 1851, *Investigator* had not found Franklin and the ship had not completed the passage, despite McClure's attempts. He sailed around the northwest corner of Banks Island, entering the strait that would one day bear his name, following the coastline, under constant threat from the floes of ice offshore. It was then, on September 23, seeking shelter from the menacing icy waters, that he came upon his misnamed Mercy Bay and its prominent sandbank.

They entered Mercy Bay driven by broken fog, snow, and descending darkness and grounded on Providence Pointshoal. They made the decision to winter in the following days, after dislodging the ship from the shoal. Did he have to take shelter there and then? Given the advanced stage of the navigation season, he would have otherwise risked wintering on the open pack.

Dr. Armstrong, the ship's surgeon, thought McClure should not have chosen to winter in Mercy Bay. He saw it as a trap. Instead, he thought that they should try to make Winter Harbour or another point farther east. He noted in his account that a few days after the decision to stay in Mercy Bay for the winter, they learned of open water nearby.

While Armstrong thought McClure's decision negligent, a more sympathetic Neatby saw compassion; he argued that this was one time that McClure put the interests of his men, depleted as they were, above his vaulting ambition. Neatby also noted yet another irony in this tale: had McClure been less sympathetic to his men's condition and pressed on, he might have completed the voyage within a few months. He would have claimed his prize and spared himself and his men the agony of their extended Arctic exile. Whatever the mercurial captain's motives — fear, prudence, empathy, exhaustion — it was a terribly fateful decision. Once *Investigator* sailed into Mercy Bay that brisk autumn day, it would sail no more.

GETTING HOME

FOR THE NEXT YEAR AND A HALF — FROM THE autumn of 1851, when *Investigator* first landed in Mercy Bay, until the spring of 1853, when help arrived — this was less a mission of rescue and discovery than one of endurance and survival. The first winter at Mercy Bay — with the men on two-thirds rations, supplemented by whatever game they could kill — was hard but bearable, given what was to come.

By the time they were ready to spend their second winter, which McClure realized would be their fate on September 9, 1852, things were dire. That winter was a horror. The temperature plunged to -65 degrees Fahrenheit (-54°C), the lowest ever recorded by any expedition. The daily ration had been reduced again, and the men were down to one meal a day. Some were found rifling through the previous winter's garbage heap. Many were weak with scurvy. Armstrong, the ship's surgeon, told McClure, again, that he didn't think the men were up to the missions that he had

ordered. They will die, he said. "It had no effect," Armstrong wrote in his journal.

Then, the next spring, deliverance. On April 6, 1853, as McClure was preparing to send out his beleaguered men on their impossible separate journeys into a forbidding wilderness, as workmen on the deck were making a coffin for a dead mate, the crew saw something on the ice. The moment was electric. A muskox? A caribou? The crew had seen no other human being in twenty-two months, and there was doubt that they would ever see another in "their desperate and hopeless situation," as the captain described it. But then, approaching them across the white land, was a lone figure, face blackened from his cooking lamp. He appeared to be from another world, and to these aching, incredulous souls, he might well have been. "Had he but given a glimpse of a tail or a cloven hoof, we should have assuredly taken to our legs," wrote McClure. "As it was, we gallantly stood our ground, and had the skies fallen upon us, we could hardly have been more astonished then when the dark-faced stranger called out...."

"I am Lieutenant Pim of the ship *Resolute*," he said, "Captain Kellet is in her at Dealy Island." Pim had found a note on a cairn, left by McClure on his trek to Winter Harbour in 1852, and here he was.

On board *Investigator*, the news ignited a strange and wondrous scene. The sickly sprang up from their beds. The workmen dropped their tools. The healthy forgot their trials. Tears of ecstasy flowed. "All was surprise, joy, animation and uproar," recalled Miertsching. Suddenly, their long night was receding. A roman candle had lit up their dark sky.

They were found, yes — but they were not yet free. Still weak and hungry, the men had to make their way over the ice to the ships, some 40 to 50 miles (65–80 km) away. In the next two days, two men died. They were told to leave all possessions behind, even their journals, which saddened Miertsching. It took him and his party sixteen days to reach HMS *Resolute*. It was now May 1853.

The last of *Investigator*'s crew did not arrive at Dealy Island until June, where they boarded *Resolute* and HMS *Intrepid*. One of the ships had been turned into a hospital. Meanwhile, Captain McClure and the crew removed provisions from *Investigator* and created a cache on the shore for future expeditions, a decision with repercussions for the region's indigenous people. In August, with the crew of *Investigator* on board, *Resolute* and its consort *Intrepid* were released as the ice broke up.

Only 100 miles (160 km) later, off Cape Colborne, they were caught in ice again, and forced to spend the winter. For the crew of *Investigator*, it was their fourth year in the cold, though this was easier than the previous two winters. By May 1854, the ships were still in the ice, and the crews of *Investigator, Resolute,* and two other ships made their way on foot to *North Star* for the voyage back to England. On August 26, they set sail, arriving home in October.

McClure was hailed as the discoverer of a northwest passage, for he and his crew had indeed circumnavigated the Americas. He claimed the prize of £10,000. He did not achieve this by water, as he had hoped; his passage was achieved through a combination of sail and sledge. Moreover, it may well be that a detached party of the Franklin expedition had identified the passage back in 1847, although Franklin himself may not have lived to learn of it.

And what of *Investigator*? In April 1854, a sledge party returned to the ship for a last time. It was *still* locked in the ice, heeling 10 degrees to starboard, but intact.

The party collected some personal items, though not Miertsching's journals, which could not be found. Some suggest that McClure did not want his or any other competing chronicle published (overtaken by an attack of conscience, however, McClure did invite Miertsching to reconstruct his account from his own journals, which the missionary did.) The final party removed more of the ship's provisions, increasing the cache left on shore. This was the last time Europeans would see *Investigator* afloat. On some unknown day, against some unknown force, it slipped beneath the waters of the Polar Sea.

PART TWO

INVESTIGATOR FOUND

THE INITIAL DISCOVERY

WHILE THERE WOULD BE OTHER EXPLORATORY expeditions in the 1850s after *Investigator*, the age of exploration had faded by early in the next century. Meanwhile, silent and oblivious, *Investigator* lay in its watery grave. In the world above, the sun set on the British Empire. Colonies became countries; one of them was Canada, which was formed less than a decade and a half after the crew of *Investigator* came home.

By the early twenty-first century, Mercy Bay remained an indentation in Banks Island, the western-most isle in the Canadian Arctic Archipelago. Its shores (though not its sea floor or waters) fell within Aulavik National Park, created in the Northwest Territories in 1992. The park brought these fragile northern lands under the protection of the federal government, part of a commitment to protecting and celebrating Canada's natural and historical heritage that began with the establishment of Banff National Park in Alberta in 1885.

While archaeologists had visited the region from the 1950s, it remained largely unexplored. In the late 1990s, Parks Canada began monitoring the area. Later, its archaeologists began making the case for searching for *Investigator*, hailing the benefits that its discovery might yield for anthropology, archaeology, and history.

Accordingly, Parks Canada decided to launch a full archaeological survey of the area. The purpose: to find *Investigator* and, if successful, to determine its condition on the seabed. Other goals included finding the graves of its three sailors buried nearby and learning more about the cache of provisions the crew had left on shore when they abandoned the ship. Once again, a search party would look for *Investigator*, 157 years after it had been abandoned.

The task would not be easy. Mercy Bay hadn't moved any closer to settled Canada; it was still at 74 degrees north latitude, 850 kilometres north of the Arctic Circle. It was still framed by high bluffs and that prominent sandbar, and it was still, even in the age of global warming, almost as impassable as it had been more than a century and a half ago. The reality was that the ice of Mercy Bay almost never melted, as McClure and his men had bitterly learned.

But now, in 2010, the mission was scientific rather than humanitarian. It would require a high level of expertise and equipment, using the instruments of the twenty-first century to find and recover the artifacts of the nineteenth century. It was still a risk. For these modern investigators in search of the ship, like those sailing on *Investigator* in search of Franklin, it might all come to nothing. This was no sure thing, much as the editorialists at *The Globe and Mail* and other sceptics argued otherwise.

"We believe that HMS *Investigator* is still in Mercy Bay," declared Ryan Harris, a senior underwater archaeologist at Parks Canada, shortly before he and the team of terrestrial and underwater archaeologists, scientists, and surveyors left for Aulavik in July 2010. They planned to spend twelve days combing its icy waters. Later that summer, they also planned to search for *Erebus* and *Terror*, Franklin's ships, in another part of the Arctic Archipelago.

They were more hopeful of finding *Investigator*. "We have more specific information to go on," said Harris.

There were the contemporaneous journals and diaries of the voyage, for example, as well as the testimony of the Inuvialuit, who for years had taken and used the copper, iron, and wood from the cache left on the island.

Still, there was no certainty that the ship would be there. Almost anything could have happened to it in the course of 157 years. *Investigator* could have drifted out of the bay and found itself carried by the currents (as had happened to another British ship) and been smashed to pieces elsewhere in the Arctic Ocean. It could have been hauled away by American whalers, as a report in *The Buffalo Daily News* suggested in 1908 (however farfetched that scenario). And even if it did sink to the bottom of Mercy Bay, as Harris believed, what would be left of it? After all this time, it seemed likely that the ice would have pulverized and shattered it or else scoured it clean. The scientists would soon find out, and astonishingly, sooner than they thought.

On July 22, 2010, the scientists arrived at Mercy Bay. It was hard to reach, even by air. First, they had to take a Twin Otter aircraft from Inuvik to Sachs Harbour, a two-hour flight. Then they flew another hour to Polar Bear Cabin, east of Castel Bay. From there, they took a helicopter to Mercy Bay, another half hour. It took four planes to transport the team, their fuel, and their gear, much of which was full of sand from sitting on a windswept airstrip during an Arctic gale.

Once there, they set up a tented camp in a place of polar bears and muskoxen, whose numbers have exploded in the region in recent years. Fresh water had to come from other parts of the island by helicopter. Because the group might be delayed by inclement weather for several days, they would need extra supplies. The team was laden with sophisticated equipment for its underwater survey. That included a side-scan sonar system, to find objects on the seabed, as well as a remotely operated vehicle, to be dropped in the water to shoot video. The crew used an inflatable 19-foot (6-metre) black Zodiac and stockpiled 880 litres of fuel. On this expedition, the plan was to take only pictures; divers would probe the wreck the following year, if they had the good fortune to find it.

Initially, the conditions discouraged Harris; when he flew into the bay on July 22, he saw that the ice had returned. Only a week earlier, it had been clear. But in between, a gale had pushed the ice into the bay. So it was with the capricious ice. Had the ice relented for only a moment for *Investigator* itself, these latter-day explorers in a motor boat with laptop computers and all the other Jules Verne wizardry of the future would have had nothing to seek and nothing to find.

Given the mercurial Arctic weather, the team didn't know how much time they would have to search. They hoped for ten days, and they were prepared to spend longer. The plan was to examine the most likely parts of Mercy Bay — the middle third — some 22 kilometres long by 7 or 8 kilometres wide. To do that, they would drag a sonar towfish, which looks like a stainless-steel torpedo, sending back its findings from the ocean floor, relaying them to a computer screen above.

On July 24, two days after their arrival, Harris and two colleagues set out on the bay for the first time. This was their first real opportunity, and they were testing the equipment. The ice had partly receded, though the area of their survey was still limited. The skies were overcast and gray. They would navigate through packs of ice, dragging a tow cable, looking out for polar bears. It was, as Harris recalls, a "challenging" environment, which made him anxious and testy.

Harris was handling remote sensing, monitoring a computer perched on his lap, while relaying instructions to Jonathan Moore, his colleague, who was navigating the boat. At the same time, John Lucas, the park manager, was watching for polar bears. Just three minutes after they deployed the sonar, Harris saw an image on his screen; it was a suspicious feature on the sea floor, something that stood out from the muddy bottom. He thought something was there, but he had to make sure. "If this is wreckage," he thought, "surely there must be more. I need to see it from another angle." After all, they had been searching for only three minutes. *Three minutes*. So, when *Investigator* first appeared beyond all doubt under the Arctic sky, there was no eureka moment. There was no exclamation or celebration, no handshakes or high-fives.

Harris and his crew bore down for the next two hours. They made more passes through the serpentine channels between the ice in order to confirm their sensational discovery. It seemed at first as if there was an anomaly on the screen. Was this really it?

If Harris was all business ("I still wanted to take a few measurements from the sonar data in order to be absolutely positive about identification"), Marc-André Bernier, chief of underwater archaeology at Parks Canada, was moved when Harris later called him in Ottawa by satellite phone to tell him the team had succeeded. "We were jubilant," he recalls. They had done it: they had found *Investigator*. It had been a walk in the park. After all the extensive and meticulous preparations, who would have thought it would happen that way?

But there it was, 450 metres offshore, in water so clear and shallow that the ship's outline was visible from the surface when the sun came out, which it did on subsequent days. *Investigator* was sitting upright, cloaked in silt. Its three masts were gone and its decks were littered with broken rails, shattered beams, and parts of fittings. Remarkably, the ship lay in only 8 metres of water to the top of the wreck and 11 metres to the ocean floor. There was a thin layer of sediment covering the ship. On the whole, it was in better shape than expected. To see the image and then the pictures was, for Harris and the other explorers, absolutely surreal.

For the archaeologists, the stars had been aligned — the mild temperatures, clear skies, retreating ice — but the success of the mission was more than good luck. The team had prepared for more than a year. The weather and the ice it could not control. But assembling the equipment, rehearsing procedures, planning their assault — everything they could control, they had. They had expected to spend two weeks plying the bay for sixteen hours a day. Astoundingly, they found the wreck on the first pass!

It was almost too easy, Harris allows, leading the inevitable critics to suggest that they always knew it was there, as if they were simply confirming the obvious. "That's preposterous," Harris bristles. If the discovery of *Investigator* was an overnight success, it had been a long time in the making. Later in the evening, following the discovery, Harris pondered what had happened that day. When he walked the gravel beach under the midnight sun, he understood the significance. "In anthropological terms, this is a very important shipwreck," he says. "It is quite significant." He noted, for example, the impact of *Investigator* on the Inuit, who had made extensive use of the copper and iron that they harvested from the ship's cache stores to supplement their material culture. As reported to Vilhjalmur Stefansson, who led the 1913–18 Canadian Arctic Expedition which visited Mercy Bay and had contact with the people of Victoria Island, the Inuit made regular visits to the cache site to quarry materials for a generation or more.

Meanwhile, the team of terrestrial archaeologists, led by Henry Cary, was also having a successful outing; while surveying with a magnetometer, it found the graves of the three seamen buried on shore near the ship. From the coffin-shaped outlines and the intact permafrost, they felt there is good reason to believe that the actual bodies are there. Out of respect, the graves were left undisturbed. They also mapped the cache site, which indeed indicated extensive salvaging by the Inuit.

It was a hugely successful expedition, witnessed, in part, by the federal Minister of the Environment, Jim Prentice. He flew in for the latter stages, boarded the Zodiac, and saw *Investigator* for himself.

A CLOSER EXAMINATION

IN JULY 2011, THEIR APPETITE WHETTED BY THE extraordinary discovery the previous summer, a team of Parks Canada archaeologists returned to Mercy Bay. In 2010 they had found, measured, and imaged *Investigator*, capturing it on four hours of underwater video. Now they were planning another amphibious expedition of about two weeks. On land, Henry Cary and his team would continue documenting the cache and dig an exploratory trench. Meanwhile, in the water, six archaeological divers (including one from the U.S. National Parks Service), led by Ryan Harris, would dive on the wreck for the first time. Their mission was to map the ship in detail, assess its structural integrity, probe its archaeological potential, inspect it closely, and recover some historical objects or artifacts of commemorative value.

This was no small undertaking. Because of the remoteness of the site — still one of the most distant, difficult places on earth, the relative warmth of summer and recent effects of global warming notwithstanding — everything, once again, had to be transported by air.

Again the workhorse was the Zodiac. There were two of them this time — one to act as the dive platform for the underwater team, the other as a safety boat and shuttle, ferrying equipment to and from shore. In their scientific arsenal, the team of explorers employed technology that would have staggered their Victorian counterparts.

Their most sophisticated instrument was a high-tech underwater laser scanner prototype developed in Waterloo, Ontario. The laser scans the surface of the sunken vessel and produces a three-dimensional digital image of the ship. Because of uncooperative water conditions, however, the device couldn't be deployed effectively in Mercy Bay, so the crew used sector scanning sonar and photo mosaics to map the wreck. HD video and a point-of-view inspection camera inserted through ruptures in the ship's upper deck complemented the documentation. Innovative stereo photogrammetry methods, produced in cooperation with Queen's University after returning from the field, yielded stunning results. Beyond that, though, a lot of the work was decidedly low-tech: hand mapping, wood sampling, and other laborious manual tasks.

Ultimately, though, the mission was about human beings working in difficult but manageable conditions. The divers, wearing thick dry suits and full-face masks against icy water, which averaged about 2 degrees Celsius, made some 100 forays over nine days. That was about how long Mercy Bay could be counted on to be clear enough of ice to allow exploration (though it actually remained open for several more weeks that summer).

For reasons of safety, the divers would go down in pairs, sometimes two teams at a time. They would stay under for sixty to seventy-five minutes. It was cold, and the divers could feel it, particularly in their numbing hands. Each of them would dive two or three times a day, the entire team generating some twelve to eighteen hours of underwater exploration a day. Up in the Zodiac, a dive supervisor would track the divers' whereabouts, assisted by a standby diver. From the shore, a wildlife monitor, armed with a rifle, would watch for polar bears, which feed where the seals gather on ice floes. Because the ship

was close to the surface and the weather held, the divers were able to see and do much as they explored the ship.

The first into the water were Harris and his colleague, Jonathan Moore; it was around 10 p.m. The time scarcely matters when there is light all day and night (one of the dives took place at 3 a.m.). They were eager to get diving after some delays, and when they did, the scene did not disappoint. Says Harris: "We took to the water as soon as we could. You never know when the wind will shift and bring in more ice. It was overcast. Then, a stately ship emerges from the gloom."

He and Moore swam the perimeter of the ship, taking in what was there. It was a reconnaissance trip. Every dive was intended to set up the next. It was all business for these professionals, another day in the Arctic office. But at a certain moment, amid the cold, the equipment, and the task, there was euphoria. "There was an initial moment," says Harris, "when I first laid eyes on the side of the ship, after it first came into view in the darkness. It is a truly exhilarating feeling being in direct contact with the past. Hovering over the quarter deck, for example, this is where the senior officers made life-and-death decisions." Other dives followed.

What did they find? On the ship's decks, there was a leather shoe, largely intact, and two partial ones.

This raises the question: To whom did these belong? Those who survived? One of those who lies in the nearby grave? The divers also found fittings (a wooden horn cleat, which would have belayed one of the ship's riggings, as well as a double-sheave pulley and a copper alloy bolt to fasten the ship's timbers.) There were also copper hull plates and a piece of insulating felt.

The most dramatic of the items retrieved from *Investigator* was the percussion side-lock musket, bearing the date 1842, a relic of another age. This was the kind of musket that the crew of *Investigator* carried when they went out on the ice and hunted for game, which was key to their survival. In all, the divers recovered sixteen artifacts. These now sit in tanks in a preservation facility in Ottawa, under the care of Flora Davidson, a leading conservator. Showing them to a visitor, she treats each of the items as if it were a baby. There are plans to put the artifacts on display.

Then, of course, there were the other less exciting but still bountiful samples of wood, iron, and copper, as well as flora and fauna. The purpose here was to assess the physical condition of the wreck, its stability, and its future. The conservators monitor corrosion, erosion, and the general level of deterioration of the wreck. That the ship is in cold water, that there is relatively little light,

that it is in a sheltered bay, and that it has lasted this long suggests that it is likely to last a long time into the future.

After *Investigator* was discovered in 2010 and documented in 2011, there was no mission to Mercy Bay in 2012. Yet the archaeologists and the scientists of the Canadian Coast Guard, the Canadian Hydrographic Service, and the Canadian Space Agency did continue their search, which also took place in both of the previous summers, for Franklin's ships. They promise to keep looking in the years ahead.

Here then, is the final, modern irony in the saga of *Investigator* and John Franklin's mysterious voyage. Having found *Investigator*, which was lost trying to find Franklin, the search for Franklin, more than a century and a half later, continues.

BIBLIOGRAPHY

Armstrong, Alexander. *A Personal Narrative of the Discovery of the North-West Passage: with numerous incidents of travel and adventure during nearly five years' continuous service in the Arctic regions while in search of the expedition of Sir John Franklin*. London: Hurst and Brackett, 1857.

Grant, Shelagh D. *Polar Imperative: A History of Arctic Sovereignty in North America*. Toronto: Douglas & MacIntyre, 2010.

McClure, Robert. *The Discovery of the Northwest Passage*. Edited by S. Osborn. London: Longman, Brown, Green and Longmans 1856. Reprint, Edmonton: Hurtig, 1969.

Miertsching, Johann. *Frozen Ships: The Arctic Diary of Johann Mierstching, 1850–1854*. Translated and edited by L.H. Neatby. Toronto: Macmillan, 1967.

Payton, Brian. *The Ice Passage: A True Story of Ambition, Disaster, and Endurance in the Arctic Wilderness*. Toronto: Doubleday Canada, 2009.

Sandler, Martin W. *Resolute: The Epic Search for the Northwest Passage and John Franklin, and the Discovery of the Queen's Ghost Ship*. London: Sterling, 2008.

HISTORICAL
IMAGES

LEFT: This sketch shows S.G. Cresswell, a member of the *Investigator* crew who was the ship's illustrator.

MIDDLE: Captain Sir Robert J. Le Mesurier McClure.

RIGHT: Daguerrotype of Johann August Miertsching, 1854.

The Arctic Council Discussing the Plan of Search for Sir John Franklin for Submission to the Lords of the Admiralty: An Historical Picture, painted by Stephen Pearce and dedicated to Lady Franklin. Note that a portrait of Franklin hangs on the wall behind the men.

Daguerrotype of Sir John Franklin in uniform, taken before he left on his fateful mission in 1845.

This painting shows *Enterprise* and *Investigator* being towed through the
Strait of Magellan in 1850 (by the steam tug HMS *Gorgon*). The mountains
of Tierra del Fuego loom to the south, with glaciers touching the sea.

One in a series of paintings of the expedition by Lieutenant Gurney Cresswell, one of the officers on board *Investigator*. This watercolour depicts the sighting of land in the Prince of Wales Strait on September 6, 1850.

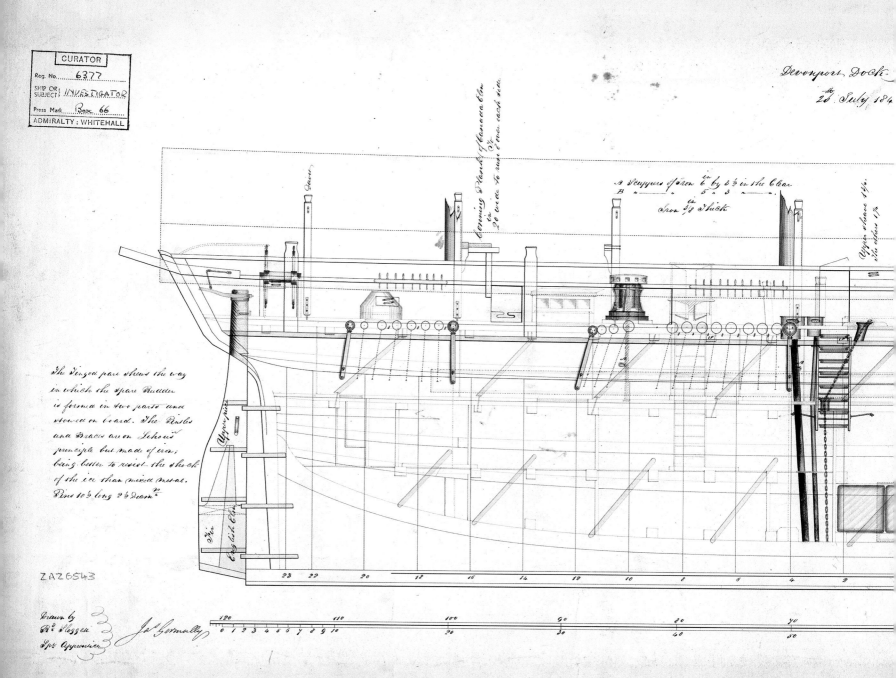

Devonport Dock.

25 July 186

A Scuppers of Iron 6 by 3½ in the Clear
B " 5 " 3 "
Iron ⅜ Thick

The Tinged part shews the way
in which the spare Rudder
is formed in two parts and
stowed on board. The Rinles
and Braces are on Sehou's
principle but made of iron;
being better to resist the shock
of the ice than mixed metal.
Pins 10½ long 2½ diam.

ZAZ6543

23 22 20 18 16 14 12 10 8 6 4 2

120   110   100   90   80   70
0 1 2 3 4 5 6 7 8 9 10   20   30   40   50

Drawn by
R. Slogger
Spr Apprentice

J. Connolly

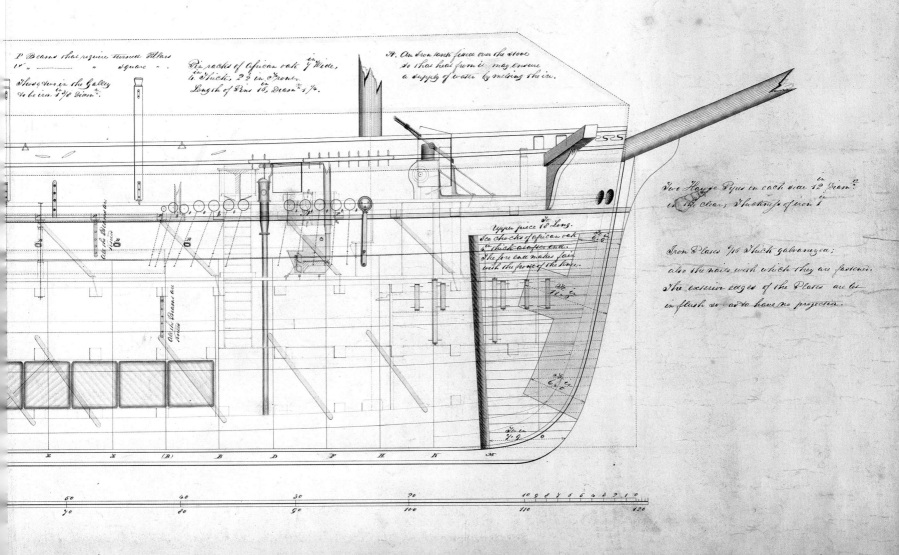

S. 6837.

Profile Draught of the inboard works of the Investigator as fitted

for the Arctic Expedition at Mess.rs ~~Hagens~~ Greens' Yard Blackwale. April 1848.

P. Beams that require turned Pillars

Pin racks of African oak 7 Wide,

A. An Iron tank fixed over the stove so that heat from it may ensure a supply of water by melting the ice.

Two Hawse Pipes in each side 12 Diam. in the clear, & thickness of iron 1.

Iron Plates 7/16 Thick galvanized; also the nails with which they are fastened. The exterior edges of the Plates are let in flush so as to have no projection.

This ship's plan shows an in-board profile. Subsequent pages show orlop, lower- and upper-deck plans, and a cross-section of *Investigator*.

Devonport Dock-Yard

26 July 1848

Elevation of Store Room.

Elevation of the Fitments of the Slop Room.

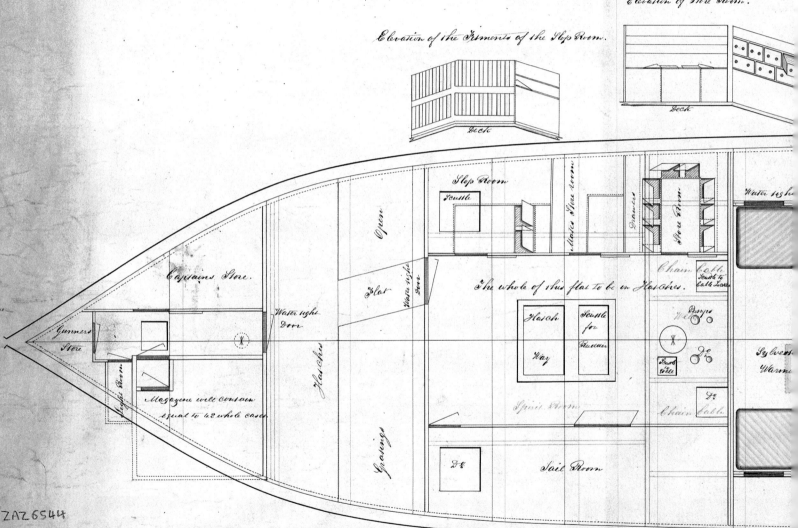

Deck

Deck

Slop Room

Scuttle

Mates Store Room

Drawers

Store Room

Water tight

Chain Cable

Scuttle to Cable Lockers

Open

Flat

Water tight Door

The whole of this flat to be in Hatches.

Captains Store.

Water tight Door

Pumps

Well

Hatch

Way

Scuttle for Rudder

Gunners Store

Hatches

Scuttle Well

Do

Chain Cable

Sylvester Warming

Magazine Room

Spirit Room

Do

Gratings

Magazine will contain equal to 42 whole cases.

Do

Sail Room

ZAZ 6544

Drawn by
R⁰ Slogges
Shipt Apprentice

Ja Gormally

S. 6837

Plan of the Orlop-Deck of the Investigator as fitted
the Arctic Expedition at Messrs. Wigrams' Yard Blackwall. April 1848
Greens'

Port side only fitted with battens for Boatswains Store.

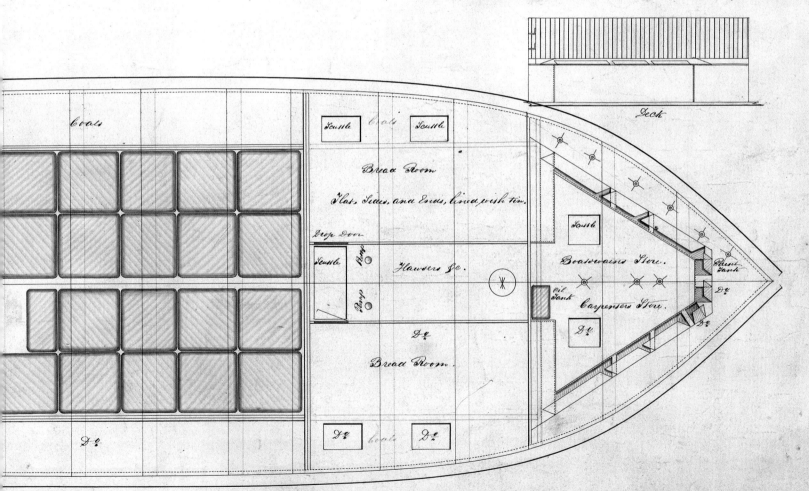

Deck

Coals

Coals

Scuttle Coals Scuttle

Bread Room

Flat, Sides, and Ends, lined with tin.

Drop Door

Scuttle Pump

Hawsers &c.

Scuttle

Boatswains Store.

Paint Tank

Pump

Oil Tank

Carpenters Store.

Do.

Do.

Do.

Do.

Bread Room.

Do.

Coals

Do.

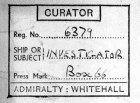

Devonport Dock-Yard
to
26 July 1848

Plan of the Lower-Deck
At Mess.rs Wigram
Greens'

Elevation of the Drawers
in the Captain's Steward's cabin.

Elevation of Bookcase
and Cupboard.

Elevation of the Tables
and Drawers in the
Captain's Cabin.

Elevation of the portable
bed place and drawers
in the officers Cabins.

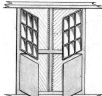

Deck

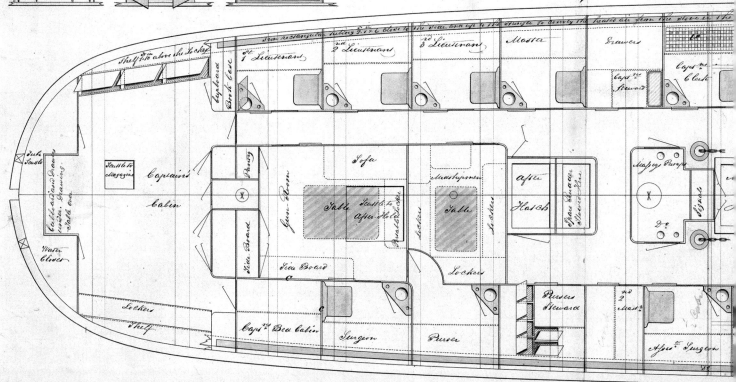

The fore and side Bulkheads of the Captain's
Bed Cabin C.C. to be double with cork shavings
between.

Elevation of the Tunnens
Pursers Steward's Cabin.

ZAZ6545

Drawn by
R.d Slaggers
Sp.t Apprentice

J.s Gormully

6837.—

...igator as fitted for the Arctic Expedition

...lackwall. April 1848.

A covering of boiler felt is put upon the sides
quite fore and aft, and upon that a lining of 3/4 in
fir board. (The edges matched.)

Elevation of the Cupboard and Coal-Box.

Deck

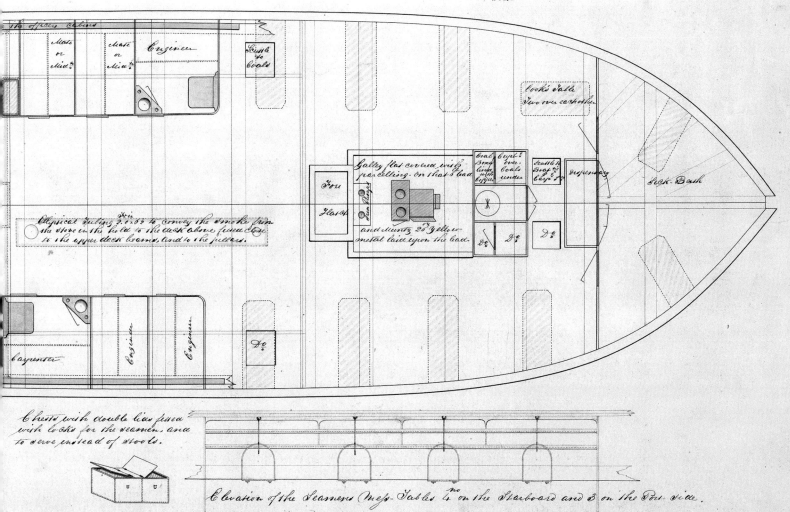

The officers cabins

Mate or Midt.   Mate or Midt.   Engineer   Scuttle to Coals

Cook's Table
Two over each other

Galley flat covered with
parcelling, on that a lead

coal
Bread
lined
with
copper

Cupt.
over
coals
under

Scuttle
Boat's
Coals

Dispensary

Sick-Bath

Fore
Hatch

Sun Rays

and Muntz 20 Yellow
metal laid upon the lead

Do.   Do.   Do.

Elliptical tubing 9 x 6.3 to convey the smoke from
the stove in the hold to the deck above, fixed close
to the upper deck beams, and to the pillars.

Carpenter   Engineer   Engineer   Do.

Chests with double lids fitted
with locks for the seamen, and
to serve instead of stools.

Elevation of the Seamens Mess-Tables 4 on the Starboard and 3 on the Port side.

Devonport Dock-Yard
26 July 1848

Plan of the Inve...

At Mess.rs Wigram's
Grans...

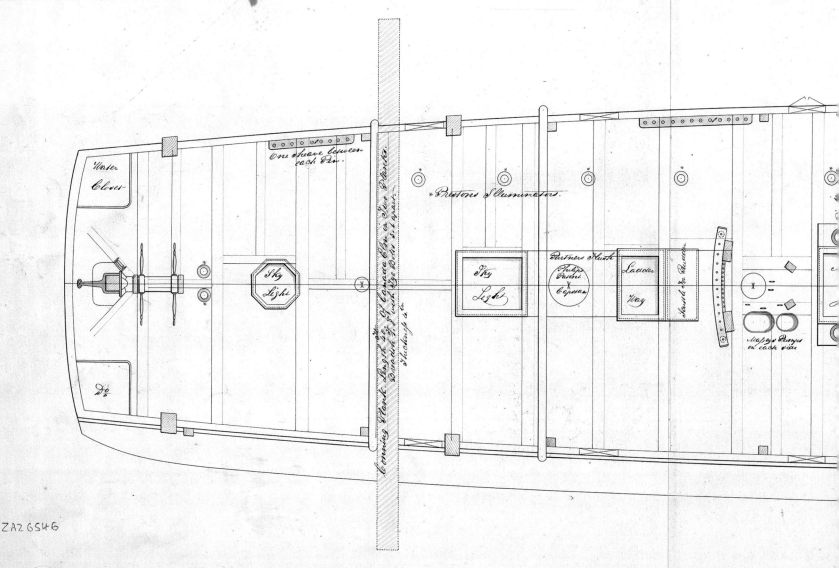

Water Closet

D.o

One sheave between each Pin.

Sky Light

Coming Stock Length &c of Canvas Plan or Iron Plank. Breadth of Flush Eye Bolts 2.6 part. Tacklings &c

✱ Prestons Illuminators.

Sky Light

Partners Hirth Philips Patent ✱ Capsean

Ladder Way

Hand to Pumps

Massey Pumps on each side

ZA2GS46

Drawn by
R.d Floggen
Sp.t Apprentice   Ja.s Gormully

6837.—

...per Deck as fitted for the Arctic Expedition

...ckwall. April 1848.

A. A piece cut out over the scuppers
   to clear the butts.

Plan of the upper part.
Sided 6"

Riding Chocks fitted each side of the Windlass for support
when at anchor. a, b to unship when required, b
to gain 2½ going down so as to be easily removed.

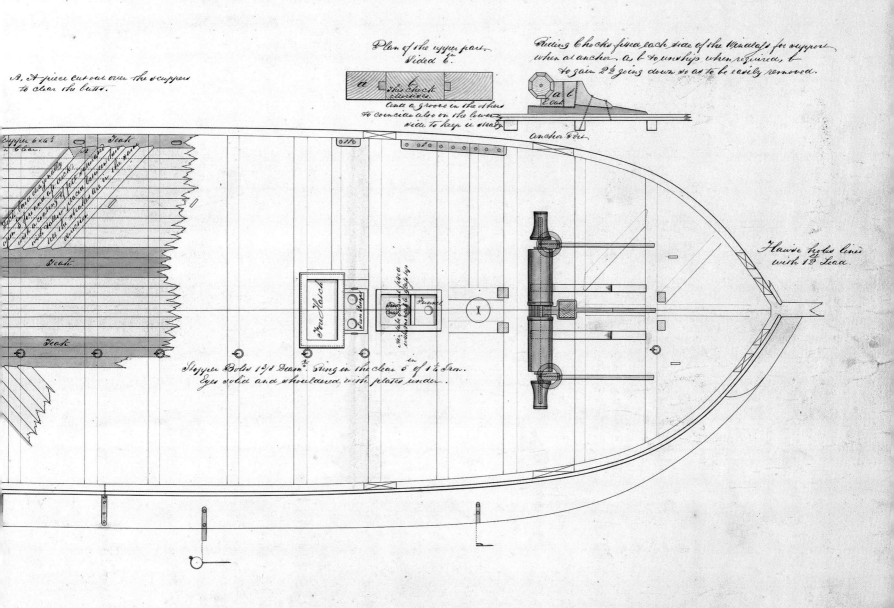

Scupper 6×4½
to clear.   Teak

a   b
This Chock
slivvises
And a groove in the others
to coincide also on the lower
side to keep it steady.

Anchor Tier

Teak

Teak

Hawse holes lined
with 12 Lead.

Fore Hatch

Funnel

Stopper Bolts 1⅜ Diam. Ring in the clear 5" of 1¼ Iron.
Eyes solid and shouldered with plates under.

S. 6837

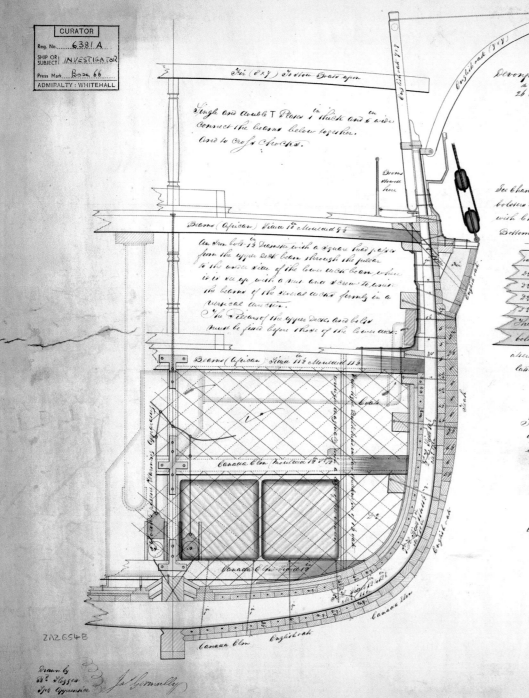

Devonport Dock-Yard   Midship Section of the Investigator
26 July 1848   as fitted for the Arctic Expedition
   at Mefs.rs Wigrams' Yard Blackwale. April/48.
   Greens

5in (8×7) Festoon Beams upon

Single and double T Plates 1in thick and 6in wide
Connect the beams below together.
And to cross Chocks.

Beams (African) Sided 10in Moulded 9¾

An iron bolt 1¾in Diameter with a square head passes
from the upper Deck beam through the pillar
to the under side of the lower deck beam, where
it is set up with a nut and screw to secure
the beams of the several decks firmly in a
vertical direction.
The Pillars of the upper Deck, and bolts
must be fixed before those of the lower deck.

Beams (African) Sided 11¾in Moulded 11¾

Canada Elm Moulded 13 & 13½

Canada Elm Sided 19

See Channels extending from the aft side of the hawse
bolsters to the quarters, filled in solid underneath
with Chocks of oak and fir alternately.
Bottom felt between the joints.

These thick strakes have two short
bolts 15in in length, and two through bolts
alternately; the former 7/8 and the
latter 1in Yellow metal.

Two circular holes are of 6in Diameter
as near the keelson as possible are in
each of the watertight bulkheads to allow
a free passage for the water, fitted with
a sheet iron plate sliding in a mixed metal
groove, and lifted from the deck with a handle,
as per sketch.

In 1½ English oak bulkhead in two thicknesses
placed diagonally, and nailed to each other.
the upper part let into the beams, and
the lower part secured to the ceiling, caulked
on both sides so as to be water tight.
There is no felt or canvas of any
kind between the boards.

Drawn by
B.r Hogger
Supt Coppersmith   J. Connolly

ZAZ 654 B

These scissors and this knife were made by Inuit using iron left behind by *Investigator*'s crew. They were collected during the Canadian Arctic Expedition that took place from 1913 to 1918.

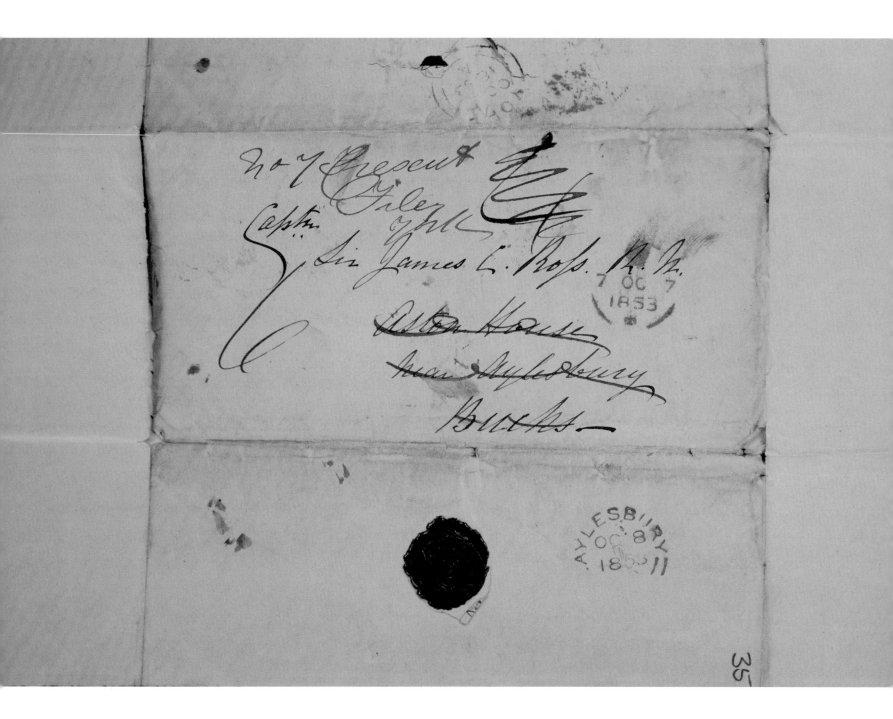

No 7 Present
Giles
Capt.
Sir James C. Ross. R. N.

7 OC 7
1853

Aston House
near Aylesbury
Bucks

AYLESBURY
OC 8
1853

A close-up of the seal also offers a view of the date.

Dispatches sent following the crew's rescue included a report detailing the discovery of Prince of Wales Strait, the final portion of the Northwest Passage (the discovery upon which McClure laid his claim). We see the actual handwriting, wax seal, and postal stamp on this envelope.

One of the dispatches from the expedition demonstrates how the captain saved paper by writing in various directions across the page. This particular document shows at least three different directions.

am disposed to think that there is no chain of Islands extending from Land to Land any between this and the Asiatic shore except a few small ones lying off the coast as we have found here, for the water is very deep, within half a mile of the shore we had seventy fathoms & a little farther there no bottom at 19 o fms. We found the tide setting from West to East, and having in the Polar Sea only six inches rise and fall at full and change, while here the mean shows two, but the greatest two or three 12.45 — I have had a wretched time and shall be truly glad when it is over, the dissensions among the officers themselves, and the importunities that I have been subjected to from each of the most young & inexperienced men I ever met with, has astounded me beyond measure owing I believe in the first place to the baneful Union of the messes where the Juniors had a majority & consequently carried every thing their own way, as none but the senior Lieutenant had ever been entitled to Gun room rank before, whose unsympathetic disposition unfitted him for keeping order, the Surgeon consequently ruled the roast who is one of the most conceited fellows I ever met having been three years in the Royal Yacht which has given him ideas of self importance which is not at all reconcilable with his position, he has given me much trouble, opposing every arrangement which I have made & his remarks upon the occasion of my telling the men last September what was my intentions with respect to sending them home, & consequently a slight reduction of provisions was so quietly created a mutiny, which might have been attended with unpleasant consequences, but the Marines with their gallant & energetic sergeant behaved like good men and true. Count is the only officer whose conduct has been exemplary & my coxswain James could arrange credit what I have had to submit I will only mention that Cresswell had the cruel impudence to tell me that "my censure or commendation was a matter of the utmost indifference to him" now really I was not prepared for this from a youngster whom in the last cruize I was aware was not considered competent to take charge of a watch — Pray do not mention any thing about my crew being disaffected, altho I have detailed the circumstance to the Admiralty, for in all other occasions I never met a finer or more energetic set & so well disposed, but they were panic struck by being told their provisions were not sufficient to support them & that the vessel ought to be laid up this year &c &c — My wife will tell Capt. Bird of our proceedings & then in I would ask you to give him a slight account & now with the kindest remembrance to dear Ross Believe me to be my dear Sir James your truly obliged & affectionate friend

Robt. Mc.Clure

This map shows part of the route taken
by *Investigator* and includes dates and
observations about the land.

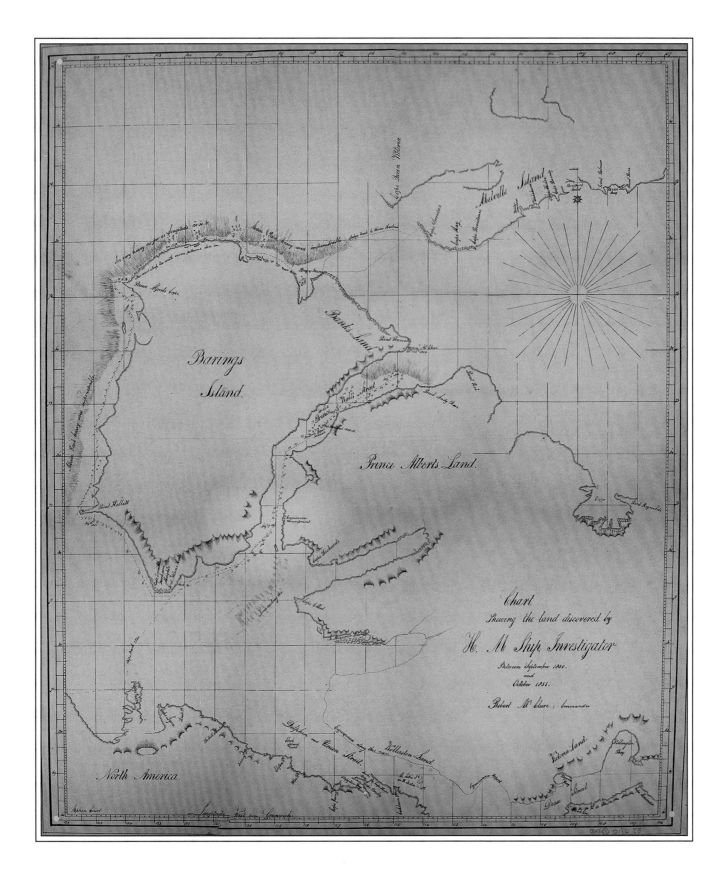

Lieutenant Cresswell painted this landscape during the journey. Under a stormy sky, *Investigator* passes close by the powerful headland on Baring Island, now Banks Island.

Here Cresswell has captured an image of
Melville Island from Banks Island.

Taken from a sketch by Cresswell, *Investigator*'s
perilous situation while wintering in the ice pack
during 1850–51 is frighteningly clear.

Captioned as "critical position of HMS *Investigator*," we see the truly precarious nature of the ship's position on the north coast of Baring Island.

This painting poignantly depicts the moment on April 6,
1853, when Lieutenant Pim of the ship *Resolute* found
Investigator trapped in the ice.

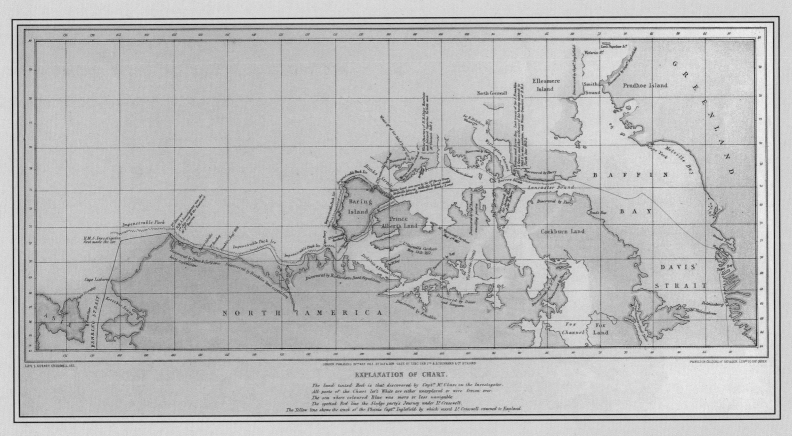

LONDON, PUBLISHED 13TH MAY 1854, BY DAY & SON, GATE ST. LINC. INN FDS & ACKERMANN & Co. STRAND

EXPLANATION OF CHART.

The land tinted Red is that discovered by Cap.t M.c Clure in the Investigator.
All parts of the Chart left White are either unexplored or were frozen over.
The sea shore coloured Blue was more or less navigable.
The spotted Red line the Sledge party's Journey under L.t Cresswell
The Yellow line shows the track of the Phœnix Cap.t Inglefield by which vessel L.t Cresswell returned to England.

This map shows the expedition's entire route in the Arctic, including that taken by the sledge party and their eventual return to England.

A portrayal of the sledge party under the command of
Lieutenant Cresswell preparing to leave *Investigator* in
Mercy Bay. The painting is dated April 15, 1853.

The caption accompanying this painting speaks for itself:
"Sledging over hummocky ice. April 1853." We begin to understand
the level of challenge and peril inherent in the journey to safety.

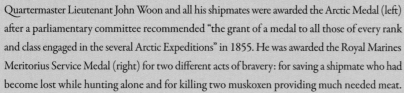

Quartermaster Lieutenant John Woon and all his shipmates were awarded the Arctic Medal (left) after a parliamentary committee recommended "the grant of a medal to all those of every rank and class engaged in the several Arctic Expeditions" in 1855. He was awarded the Royal Marines Meritorius Service Medal (right) for two different acts of bravery: for saving a shipmate who had become lost while hunting alone and for killing two muskoxen providing much needed meat.

This portrait by Jack Bridge shows Quartermaster Lieutenant John Woon in uniform. He is wearing (left to right) the Royal Marines Meritorious Service Medal, the Arctic Medal 1818–1855, and the Second China Medal 1856–60.

Members of a 1908–1909 expedition visited Banks Island and found material left on shore by the crew of *Investigator*. This image shows them examining the remains of a rope.

Ein unschuldiges Opfer der Hofrichter-Affäre an Herzkrampf gestorben.

Preis 4 Heller

Preis 4 Heller

Schriftleitung:
Wien, III/1, Seidlgasse 8
Fernsprecher 3314.
Unverlangt eingesendete
Manuskripte usw. werden
grundsätzlich, auch wenn
Rückporto beiliegt, nicht
zurückgeschickt.

Verwaltung
und
Inseraten - Aufnahme:
Wien, III/1, Hetzgasse 16
Fernsprecher 4701.

Stadtbureau
für „Kleine Anzeigen"
und Abonnements:
Wien, I., Schulerstr. 21
Fernsprecher 6211.
Abonnementspreis mit
Zustellung ins Haus für
Wien 1 Krone;
für die Provinz:
per Monat K 1.30, per
¼ Jahr K 4.50, per ½ Jahr
K 8.60, per Jahr K 18.—;
für das Ausland um die
Postdifferenz mehr.

Die Neue Zeitung

Illustriertes unabhängiges Tagblatt.

Das Blatt erscheint täglich einmal um 6 Uhr morgens. Montag erfolgt die Ausgabe um 12 Uhr mittags.

Nr. 27 — Wien, Freitag, den 28. Jänner 1910 — 3. Jahrgang

Auffindung eines verschollenen Polarschiffes.

(Text hiezu im Innern des Blattes.)

Zur Bekämpfung der öffentlichen Unsittlichkeit.

Von Hermann Roeren, geheimen Justizrat, Mitglied des deutschen Reichstages.

Bei allen Nationen der zivilisierten Welt zeigt sich seit Jahren ein sittlicher Niedergang, der erschreckend ist und mit Sorge für die Zukunft erfüllen muß. Anfänglich wurde dies von den Vertretern der modernen Ethik und Gegnern der christlichen Moralanschauung, weil nicht recht in ihre Theorien passend, bestritten. In den letzten Jahren aber ist die Vertretung der Unsittlichkeit in solchem Maße hervorgetreten, die statistischen Erhebungen haben so niederdrückende Resultate ergeben, die Standalprozesse der letzten Zeit haben einen so traurigen Einblick in den Abgrund sittlicher Verkommenheit auch in den Kreisen der sogenannten besseren Gesellschaft gewährt und eine solche Bejahung und Umwertung der Sittlichkeitsbegriffe gezeigt, daß diesen Erscheinungen gegenüber das Leugnen nicht mehr Stand zu halten vermag und von den Gegnern jetzt zugegeben wird, daß die sittliche Versuchung in erschreckendem Maße um sich greift.

Der untrüglichste Beweis für die wachsende Entsittlichung im allgemeinen liegt naturgemäß in der wachsenden Zahl der Prostituierten. Es ist eine traurige Tatsache, daß die Zahl dieser Personen in den letzten Jahren nicht allein in allen Großstädten, sondern überhaupt in allen größeren Städten ohne Ausnahme in erschreckender Weise zugenommen hat, und zwar durchwegs weit über das prozentuale Verhältnis des Zuwachses der Bevölkerung hinaus. Die Statistik ergibt dies zur Evidenz. Und doch beziehen sich die ermittelten Zahlen nur auf die sogenannte öffentliche Prostitution, also auf diejenigen Personen, die der polizeilichen Kontrolle unterstellt sind, während die Zahl derjenigen Personen, die ebenfalls der Prostitution ergeben sind, ohne aus besonderen Gründen gerade der Kontrolle unterstellt zu sein, also die sogenannte geheime Prostitution, nach den Erfahrungen, die nach dieser Richtung zu machen sind, durchschnittlich auf das sechs- bis siebenfache veranschlagt werden muß. Das sind furchtbare Zahlen, wenn man bedenkt, was hinter ihnen steckt, und daß das Treiben der Städte nach und nach auch auf die Landstädte und das ländliche Leben einwirkt und seine verderblichen Folgen dorthin durchsickern läßt!

In ungefähr gleichem Maße haben die zur gerichtlichen Aburteilung gelangenden Sittlichkeitsvergehen und -verbrechen zugenommen, und das betrübendste hiebei ist, daß diese Steigerung wesentlich auf das Konto der jugendlichen Personen kommt. Hand in Hand hiermit geht das immer weitere Umsichgreifen der Seuche der Geschlechtskrankheiten. Auf einer Versammlung von medizinischen Sachverständigen, die vor einiger Zeit in Nürnberg stattfand, berichtete ein Arzt über die in dieser Hinsicht angestellten Erhebungen und konstatierte dabei, daß der größte Prozentsatz der Infizierten auf auf die akademische Jugend falle.

Aber noch tiefer hinab greift diese Seuche, bis selbst in die Reihen der Schüler an den Gymnasien! Tatsachen hiefür liegen vor. Man kann sich darüber nicht wundern, wenn man bedenkt, daß festgestellt ist, wie schon in manchen Volks- und Elementarschulen das Gift der geheimen Sünde der Selbstschändung Verbreitung gefunden hat!

Alles das sind Erscheinungen, die den sittlichen Niedergang unseres Volkes nicht mehr als zweifelhaft gelten lassen. Und doch ist zu beachten, daß alles das, was auf diesem Gebiete in die Oeffentlichkeit dringt, was wir erfahren, was durch die Presse und die Gerichts-

This false account of *Investigator*'s discovery appeared in an
Austrian newspaper *Die Neue Zeitung* in 1910. It reads:
"Missing Polar Ship Discovered."

CONTEMPORARY
IMAGES

———

Part of the Underwater Archaeology Services team stands on a polar map on the floor of the Inuvik airport. Left to right: Thierry Boyer, Jonathan Moore, Filippo Ronca, Marc-André Bernier, Ryan Harris.

Investigator was found off the
shores of what is now Aulavik
National Park, pictured here.

The rushing waters of Mercy River Falls in Aulavik National Park provided fresh water to the team of archaeologists.

A map of the area, including Aulavik National Park and the town of Inuvik. The park is located on Banks Island in the Northwest Territories. McClure's Cache and an archaeological site from the Paleoeskimo period are both found within its boundaries. *Investigator* rests approximately 8 metres from the surface of Mercy Bay, just offshore of Aulavik National Park. Sachs Harbour is the only community on the island. Inuvik is the largest town in the western Arctic and is considered a gateway to the region.

Gyrfalcon Bluff, on the shore of
Mercy Bay, in Aulavik National Park.

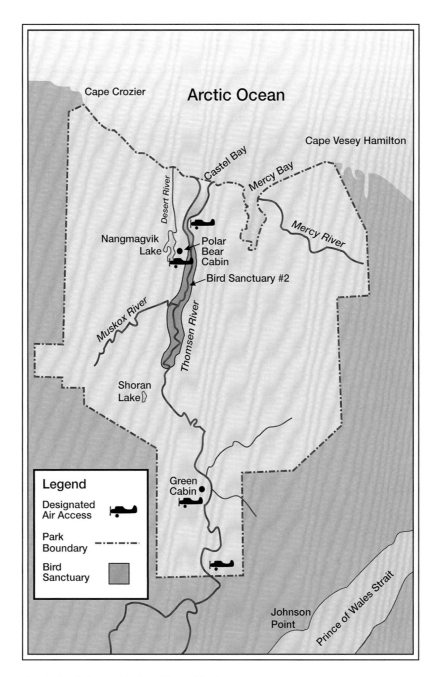

A detailed map of Aulavik National Park,
with Mercy Bay appearing near the top right.

Ryan Harris examines the davit stanchion found on the east shore of Mercy Bay. When the team first arrived in Mercy Bay in 2010, there was a fair amount of ice in the bay and they were discouraged that they could not immediately start searching the water. But this artifact, found on the land, was their first indication that they were very close to a shipwreck.

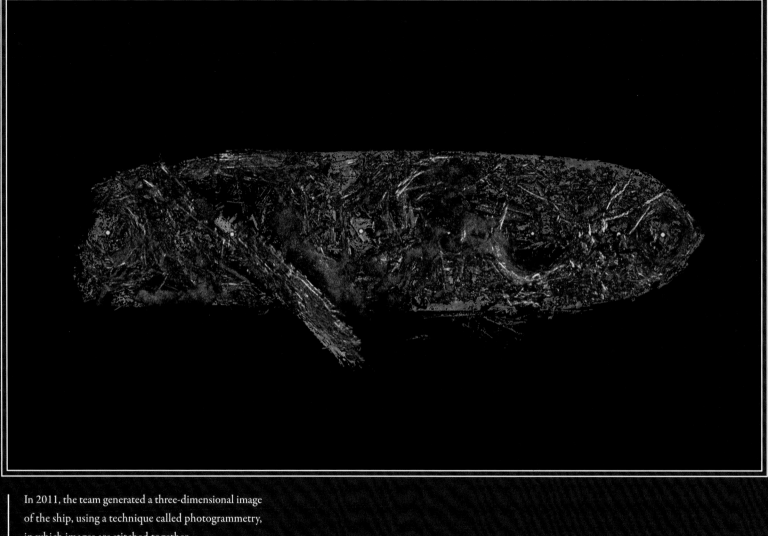

In 2011, the team generated a three-dimensional image
of the ship, using a technique called photogrammetry,
in which images are stitched together.

This underwater image shows the bow of *Investigator* as
seen from the port side, along with the anchor chain.

A close-up of *Investigator*'s stern shows
the gudgeon and draft marks.

This close-up view of the stern post shows the copper-sheeting on the starboard side. The roman numeral draught marks on the stern post were used to indicate the ship's load.

While much of *Investigator* is filled with sediment, the team was able to insert a video camera into some parts of the ship that could not be entered by divers.

Investigator was equipped with many state-of-the-art features. One of these was Gossage's "Improved Engine Pump." A pump was an essential tool on board a ship for filling casks of drinking water, extinguishing fires, and many other purposes.

This is a mosaic of the side-scan sonar imagery of Mercy Bay. Each strip in the image represents one pass made by the team towing the side-scan sonar. It was important to keep each pass as straight as possible in order to get an accurate map of the sea floor. Deep scours created by the ice are visible on the sea floor around the ship.

This long arm was carefully and painstakingly recovered from *Investigator* by a highly trained archaeological team.

The double-sheave pulley, used for rigging, was recovered from *Investigator* in relatively good condition.

From left to right, these artifacts recovered from *Investigator* include: a wooden horn cleat (around which the ropes would have been looped to secure the vessel's rigging); a copper alloy bolt used to fasten ship timbers; a leather shoe; and a double-sheave pulley block for rigging.

A leather shoe recovered from *Investigator* is just barely recognizable as such. The missionary on board, Johann August Miertsching, was a trained cobbler who may have repaired footwear for the crew members.

Henry Cary, Mervin Joe, and Joe Kudlak exca-
vate a yard truss, used to attach the yard to the
mast, found on the shore of Mercy Bay

The broad arrow — the mark of the British Royal Navy — appears clearly on this sheave fragment found on land.

A piece of rope found in a gully near the cache site. Rope belonging to the Royal Navy would include a strand of dyed wool mixed in with the stronger hemp. This "rogue's yarn," as it was known, was purposely placed and colour-coded to indicate the originating dockyard. This way, rope could be traced if necessary.

A field of barrel staves
and metal pieces.

No menace is apparent in this stunning portrait of water and
ice. Although great depth and mystery are suggested, the
overriding feature on the surface is calm.

One senses the scope of the water with its
intermittent ice floes and the barrenness
of the landscape in the distance.

A spectacular aerial view of Mercy Bay in Aulavik National Park. The barren land, outlined against the deep green of the sea, offers a hint of the majestic beauty, breadth, and depth of water that defines this place.

This photograph taken during the 2010 expedition shows the complexity of travel to this region. The crew had to travel by Twin Otter to Polar Bear Cabin, then unload all the gear, which was taken by helicopter to the base camp at Mercy Bay. Because there is no nearby source of fresh water, even it had to be brought in by helicopter from Mercy Falls.

A helicopter delivers gear to the campsite of the 2010 expedition.

Dive gear preparation on shore gives a sense
of the complexities involved in this type of
search and recovery operation.

For all its high-tech equipment and supplies, the camp at Mercy Bay in Aulavik National Park is completely dwarfed by the power and majesty of the surrounding landscape.

An aerial view of the tents stretching along the shoreline
once again emphasizes their insignificance and vulnerability
in relation to the vastness and power of the place.

John Lucas sits on shore,
gazing out at the water.

Despite all the work to be done, it was possible to find a quiet moment. Here we see crew member Joe Kudlak fishing from a growler or small piece of ice.

A member of the team carries water buckets along the shore, offering a small insight into life on the expedition.

The calm, brilliantly sunny day offers a striking juxtaposition to the clear power and force represented by the ice.

Ryan Harris, Thierry Boyer, and Mervin Joe work
together to set up the remotely operated vehicle that
captured the first video images of the wreck in 2010.

Thierry Boyer and Ryan
Harris huddle to review
video footage.

Team member Jonathan Moore stands silhouetted
on the cairn at Providence Point.

Team member Mervin Joe at work. He is using a
metal detector at the site from the Paleoeskimo
period, looking for more recent metal artifacts.

Three members of the land archaeology
team position flags showing artifact
discoveries on the cache site.

Ryan Harris, Letitia Pokiak, Henry Cary, Jonathan
Moore, Joe Kudlak, and Mervin Joe enjoy dinner in
the kitchen tent after a hard day of work.

Two laptops set up in a tent at the Mercy Bay base camp. The one on the left shows the historical ship plans of *Investigator* while the other shows imagery captured by the remotely operated vehicle.

Underwater Archaeology Service *Investigator* diving team in 2011. From left to right, back row: Brett Seymour (US National Park Service), Jonathan Moore; front row: Thierry Boyer, Marc-André Bernier, Joe Kudlak, Ryan Harris, Filippo Ronca.

Inflatable boat going to the
dive site with the crew
from CTV's *W5*.

The actual moment of discovery in
2010 as the crew surveys the depths
with the side-scan sonar.

Team member Jonathan Moore sits in the Zodiac with his
computer and other equipment. The structure beside him
holds the tow cable for the side-scan sonar.

Jim Prentice, who was Minister of the Environment at the time, was able to get a first-hand view of the ship by snorkelling on his visit to the site.

In this beautiful and dramatic underwater view, Ryan Harris from the team swims over *Investigator*'s bow.

Thierry Boyer films *Investigator*'s stern post.

The Gossage pump is examined by Marc-André Bernier.

Ryan Harris writes on a "dive slate"
while working underwater.

Archaeologists Marc-André Bernier and Ryan Harris raise a long arm rifle into the Zodiac after recovering it from *Investigator*. The team improvised and used the lid from an equipment case to support the artifact as it was being brought to the surface. While team members prepared for many eventualities, they also had to pack lightly. Because they could not predict the number and type of artifacts they would find and choose to bring back to the lab in Ottawa, they often improvised with whatever material they had on hand.

The 2010 field team poses for a photo with former Environment Minister Jim Prentice. Left to right: Mervin Joe, Jonathan Moore, Henry Cary, John Lucas, Joe Lucas, Joe Kudlak, Ryan Harris, Jim Prentice, Letitia Pokiak, Ifan Thomas, Edward Eastaugh, and Thierry Boyer.

This stunning view of the lower falls of Mercy River in Aulavik National Park is a final reminder of the power and beauty of this place that has seen so much dramatic history.

PHOTO CREDITS

The numbers on the left refer to the pages of this book. All images are under copyright unless otherwise noted and are reproduced by permission of the institutions or individuals cited below.